THE HELPER

Exploring the Enneagram Type 2

Asa Eccleston Kibilski

CONTENTS

THE WARM EMBRACE: UNDERSTANDING THE ENNEAGRAM TYPE 2 CORE

The gentle hum of a coffee shop, the soft clink of mugs, and a stranger's quiet tears – this everyday tableau embodies the world of the Enneagram Type Two, also known as The Helper. It's a world infused with deep empathy, a relentless desire to connect with others, and a near-innate ability to recognize and respond to the emotional needs of those around them. If this resonates with you, you might be a Helper.

The Essence of the Helper

At the core of the Enneagram Type Two is a fundamental desire to be loved, needed, and appreciated. Twos long to have a special place in the hearts of others and to feel irreplaceable. Their ability to perceive unspoken needs and their generous spirit make them sought-after friends, partners, and colleagues. But, behind this warm exterior often lies a nagging fear of being unlovable or unworthy if they are not helpful to others.

The driving need to be needed can make Twos experts at anticipating and fulfilling the desires of others, often to the detriment of recognizing their own needs. It's this deep-seated belief that their value lies in their helpfulness that can make it difficult for Twos to take a step back, say "no," or acknowledge their own emotional wants.

The Enneagram: A Map for Self-Understanding

The Enneagram is a dynamic personality system that goes well beyond mere categorization. It's an invitation to embrace a more profound awareness of ourselves. At its heart, the Enneagram reveals our deepest motivations, our habitual patterns, and the unique ways we interact with the world.

Unlike other personality systems, the Enneagram isn't just about labeling ourselves. It helps us understand the "why" behind our actions, thoughts, and feelings. Understanding your Enneagram type isn't about placing yourself in a box; it's about unlocking a key to self-discovery, growth, and ultimately, greater compassion for yourself and others.

Identifying as a Type Two

Some telltale signs that you may identify as an Enneagram Type Two include:

- **Empathy as a superpower:** You have an uncanny ability to read the emotions of others, often feeling what they feel before they even express it.
- **Natural caregiving:** Offering help, whether it's a listening ear, a warm meal, or a shoulder to cry on, comes effortlessly to you.
- **The need to be needed:** You derive a sense of purpose and fulfillment from being helpful and seeing your efforts make a positive impact on others.
- **Sensitivity to feedback:** Praise and recognition feel essential to your well-being, while criticism can be particularly cutting.
- **Difficulty expressing your own needs:** Putting the needs of others ahead of your own is a deeply ingrained habit.

Beyond the Stereotypes

It's important to note that while Twos are often depicted as selfless caregivers, their true motivations can be far more complex. While helping others is a defining trait, it's equally important to uncover the underlying motivations and fears that propel this behavior.

This journey into your Enneagram type is an invitation to explore questions like:

- How does your desire to be loved and needed impact your relationships and sense of self?
- Are there moments where your helpfulness becomes a way to avoid your own needs?
- Can you identify healthy and unhealthy patterns in the way you show up for others?

Embracing the Invitation

"The Helper: Exploring the Enneagram Type 2" is your guide to exploring the depths of your personality. Through the pages of this book, we'll delve into the complexities of the Type Two, unpacking the gifts, challenges, and pathways to growth inherent in this dynamic archetype.

Let this exploration be a compassionate one. It's not about fixing what is "wrong" with you; it's about embracing all of who you are, celebrating your strengths, and shedding light on areas where you can continue to grow into a more authentic and fulfilled version of yourself.

HEARTS ON FIRE: THE FEELING CENTER AND THE HELPER'S DRIVE

Imagine the human psyche divided into three distinct centers of intelligence: the Head, the Heart, and the Body. These centers dictate how we perceive the world, make decisions, and navigate our experiences. For Enneagram Type Twos, the Heart Center reigns supreme.

The Heart Center: A Wellspring of Emotion

The Heart Center, also known as the Feeling Center, is where our emotions reside. It's associated with connection, empathy, intimacy, and our deepest sense of identity. Those whose primary intelligence lies in the Heart Center lead with their feelings – their decisions, interactions, and outlook on life are heavily colored by their emotional landscape.

The other two types within the Heart Center are Type Three (The Achiever) and Type Four (The Individualist). While all three types experience the world through an emotional lens, the focus of these emotions diverges:

- **Type Two (The Helper):** Focuses on the needs and feelings of others, seeking love and appreciation through acts of service.
- **Type Three (The Achiever):** Seeks validation and admiration through achievements and external success.
- **Type Four (The Individualist):** Longs for deep connection and a sense of unique identity, often channeled through creative and emotional expression.

The Helper's Emotional Compass

For a Type Two, their emotional compass provides invaluable

insight into the needs of those around them. Their ability to tune into the feelings of others is like a superpower – they can sense a change in mood before it manifests, understand unspoken pain, and intuitively offer the right kind of support.

This profound empathy is also what fuels the Helper's overwhelming desire to connect. Twos crave meaningful bonds built on shared feelings, mutual understanding, and a genuine sense of being needed. Their hearts ache to not only know that they are loved but also to feel as though they make a tangible difference in the lives of those they care about.

The Double-Edged Sword of Emotion

However, the dominance of the Heart Center can be a double-edged sword. While deep empathy is a remarkable strength, it also makes Twos vulnerable to emotional overwhelm. They can easily absorb the burdens of others as their own, potentially leading to emotional exhaustion or neglecting their own needs in the process.

Additionally, the Helper's intense focus on love and appreciation can create a blind spot. When feelings become the primary lens for decision-making, it can sometimes overshadow objectivity and lead to a fear of expressing any emotion that might be seen as "negative" or potentially strain relationships.

The Inner Landscape of the Unhealthy Two

When a Type Two becomes unhealthy, their focus on external validation and connection can morph into a desperate need for attention and affection. Unchecked, this can manifest in behaviors like:

- **People-pleasing:** Sacrificing personal needs and boundaries to maintain the approval of others.
- **Manipulation:** Using guilt or emotional appeal to get their way.
- **Codependency:** Clinging to relationships for a sense of self-

worth and identity.

- **Pride:** Masking their own vulnerability with an illusion of selflessness and superiority.

Balancing Head and Heart

The path to growth for a Type Two lies in developing a stronger connection with the other centers of intelligence. When Twos can tap into the objectivity of the Head Center (Types Five, Six, and Seven) and the groundedness of the Body Center (Types Eight, Nine, and One), they find greater balance and resilience.

Remember, being a Heart Center type doesn't mean your emotions should rule your life. By cultivating greater self-awareness and learning to set healthy boundaries, Type Twos can harness their gifts of empathy and create fulfilling connections without compromising their own well-being.

THE WINGS OF SERVICE: EXPLORING TWOS WITH ONE AND THREE WINGS

Picture the Enneagram symbol, a circle with nine points connected by intricate lines. At the heart of the symbol lies your basic Enneagram type – the core of your personality. Yet, like colors on a painter's palette, our personalities are rarely this simple. Enter the concept of wings.

Your wings are the two Enneagram types adjacent to your primary type. These provide additional nuance and complexity, subtly influencing your traits, motivations, and how you move through the world. For our Helpers, Type Two, the possible wings are Type One (The Reformer) and Type Three (The Achiever).

The Two with a One Wing: "The Servant"

Twos with a One wing bring a dash of the Reformer's perfectionism and sense of duty to their helpful nature. There's a stronger focus on not just being helpful but ensuring things are done "the right way." Here's what this might look like:

- **Conscientiousness:** A heightened concern for fulfilling responsibilities and maintaining standards of excellence, even in acts of service.
- **The Inner Critic:** A stronger inner voice focused on correctness, potential mistakes, and a tendency to hold themselves to incredibly high standards.
- **Morality:** May have a well-defined sense of right and wrong, expressing their care by guiding others or advocating for causes they believe in.
- **Potential Tension:** The desire to help can clash with a rigid sense of how things "should" be, causing frustration when

others don't meet their expectations.

The Two with a Three Wing: "The Host/Hostess"

Twos with a Three wing possess a touch of the Achiever's ambition and desire for recognition. They are often the life of the party – sociable, outgoing, and focused on creating an air of warmth and welcome for those around them. Here's how this might manifest:

- **Charisma and Image:** Increased focus on their appearance and external presentation, a desire to be perceived as successful and well-liked.
- **Performance:** They might derive satisfaction from the positive feedback and visible results of their helpful actions.
- **Competitiveness:** A subtle competitive edge may emerge, especially when it comes to being seen as the most helpful, generous, or likable person.
- **Potential Tension:** The drive for external success could overshadow their genuine desire to help, leading to help given to receive admiration rather than from a place of pure altruism.

The Spectrum of Wings

It's crucial to remember that wings are dynamic. Some Twos might strongly identify with one wing, while others experience a more balanced blend of both. The strength of your wing can also fluctuate depending on stress levels or seasons of life.

Furthermore, wing influence is rarely simple. Here's where it gets exciting:

- **Integration:** Type Ones and Threes represent points of integration for Twos. That means understanding your wing can provide clues for growth and balance.
- **Disintegration:** Under stress, Twos may adopt less healthy traits of their wings – a Two with a One wing might become overly critical and rigid, while a Two with a Three wing

might become self-centered and image-obsessed.

Exploration and Self-Awareness

Identifying your preferred wing is about self-discovery, not fitting yourself into a new box. Consider these guiding questions:

- Do you tend to focus on being "right" or being "liked" when providing help?
- Are you more comfortable with quiet acts of service or grand gestures of generosity?
- Do you experience a strong inner critic or a desire to impress others?

Observing your thoughts, feelings, and behaviors in situations where you're being helpful will reveal your natural inclinations. Remember, there's no better or worse wing; each offers a unique lens through which to understand yourself and cultivate a more balanced, authentic version of your Helper self.

BEYOND THE MASK: THE HEALTHY AND UNHEALTHY EXPRESSIONS OF A TYPE TWO

There's a misconception about the Enneagram Type Two, The Helper: that their generosity and warmth are constant, unwavering traits. The truth is, like all Enneagram types, Twos exist on a spectrum of health. Within this dynamic spectrum, we'll explore the masks that Twos may wear, and how these reflect their underlying levels of psychological and emotional well-being.

The Spectrum of Health

Every Enneagram type ranges from unhealthy, to average, to healthy expressions. Unhealthy levels indicate a greater disconnect from the true essence of the type, with behaviors driven by deeper fears and unconscious motivations. Healthy levels demonstrate personal growth, integration of other Enneagram types, and actions aligned with the core positive qualities of the type.

The Unhealthy Two: The Masks of Neediness

When Twos slip into unhealthy levels, their underlying fear of being unwanted or unlovable amplifies. Helpfulness, once a genuine expression of care, becomes a tool to manipulate, control, or to receive love and validation they don't believe they deserve. Common unhealthy Two behaviors include:

- **Possessiveness in Relationships:** Driven by insecurity, they may become possessive of loved ones, clinging or becoming overly jealous.
- **Indirect Expression:** Unable to ask directly for their needs, they may resort to sulking, passive-aggression, or playing the victim.

- **Repressed Anger:** The 'good helper' image disallows the expression of anger, frustration, or disappointment, leading to buried resentment.
- **Pride in Servitude:** The Two may subtly take pride in their sacrifices, developing a subconscious feeling of superiority and moral righteousness.

At the lowest end of the spectrum, neediness masquerades as selflessness.

The Average Two: Balancing Need and Authenticity

The average Two represents the majority – well-meaning individuals with a genuine desire to help, yet still wrestling with their underlying need for love. They may fluctuate between:

- **Ambivalence About Needs:** Recognizing they have needs, but fearing that expressing them fully would be selfish or burdensome.
- **Selective Helpfulness:** A tendency to focus on those who offer them appreciation and validation, potentially neglecting others.
- **Moments of Clarity:** Flashes of insight where they recognize their own manipulative tendencies, but struggle to change consistently.

The average Two is on a journey of self-awareness, slowly confronting the less comfortable aspects of their personality.

The Healthy Two: Embracing Genuine Altruism

Healthy Twos embody self-acceptance and radiate warmth because they've found internal validation. They're able to give generously without expecting anything in return. Characteristics of a healthy Two include:

- **Discerning Helpfulness:** They intuit when help is truly needed and when it's better for someone to find their own way.
- **Healthy Boundaries:** The ability to say "no" with kindness, to

prioritize their own needs without guilt.

- **Acceptance of Own Needs:** They recognize they deserve love and care, asking for help when necessary.
- **Humility:** Genuine humility replaces subtle pride, they find joy in service without needing praise or recognition.

The healthy Two is the most fulfilled version of themselves, finding freedom in giving from a place of inner abundance.

The Path to Growth

Growth for a Two lies in recognizing how their desire to be needed gets in the way of authentic connection and fulfilling their own potential. Practices for Twos:

- **Embracing Your Emotions:** Learning to recognize, validate, and healthily express ALL emotions, not just the positive ones.
- **Self-Inquiry:** Asking "Why am I helping in this situation?" reveals true motivations.
- **Practice Receiving:** Accepting gifts, compliments, and help from others helps break the belief that you must earn love.

Remember: Unhealthy behaviors don't make you a bad person; they're signs that your Type Two core needs are unmet. The Enneagram is a tool for compassion - towards others AND yourself. This journey of self-exploration offers the gift of liberation – freedom from the need to perform in order to be lovable, and the joy of living wholeheartedly.

THE CRAVING FOR CONNECTION: UNDERSTANDING THE INTIMACY NEEDS OF TWOS

If the heart of a Type Two could speak, it would beat a steady rhythm of longing: "Connect with me. Know me. Need me." For Helpers, intimacy is where they feel safe, valued, and truly seen. Yet, their deep-seated fear of rejection can create a complex dance in relationships, a push-and-pull between yearning for closeness and a terror of being exposed and found unworthy of love.

What Does "Intimacy" Mean for a Two?

True intimacy stretches beyond romantic partnerships. For Twos, it exists within close friendships, family bonds, and even the sense of community they carefully cultivate. Intimacy, for a Helper, means:

- **Emotional Vulnerability:** Feeling safe enough to share their deepest fears, insecurities, and needs without fear of judgment or abandonment.
- **Feeling Indispensable:** Knowing they have a unique and irreplaceable place in someone's life, that their presence makes a tangible difference.
- **Reciprocal Care:** A sense of give-and-take, not just being the giver but also feeling nurtured, supported, and truly understood.
- **Unconditional Love:** The deep belief that they are loved fully for who they are, flaws and all, without needing to constantly prove their worth.

The Paradox of the Helper

Twos crave connection like warmth on a winter night. But the same heart that yearns for closeness can also push others away.

This paradox stems from a core belief that if someone truly knows them – the messy, imperfect parts – they won't be loved. This plays out in behaviors such as:

- **Smothering Affection:** Overwhelmed by their desire to be close, they may unintentionally push the other person away with excessive attention and caretaking.
- **Testing the Relationship:** Unconsciously creating situations to "prove" someone's love, whether through playing the victim or withdrawing affection to see if the other person fights for them.
- **Over-Adapting:** Subtly morphing their personality to match what they perceive the other person wants, sacrificing authenticity in pursuit of connection.
- **The Fear of Neediness:** Downplaying their own needs or desires, fearing that expressing them might make them seem "too much" and drive the other person away.

The Path to Healthy Connection: For Twos

The journey towards fulfilling intimacy for Twos lies in confronting their core fear of being unlovable. It's a process of learning to receive love as readily as they give it. Key practices include:

- **Befriending Your Inner Critic:** Identifying and challenging the inner voice that says you're unworthy of love and connection.
- **Self-Compassion over Perfection:** Embracing the vulnerability of being flawed and imperfect, recognizing that your worthiness is inherent.
- **Communicating Needs Directly:** Learning to express needs clearly and kindly, trusting that healthy relationships can withstand honesty.
- **Prioritizing Reciprocity:** Paying attention to the balance of give-and-take within relationships, making sure you're receiving care in return.

A Note for Those Loving a Type Two

If you love a Two, recognize that their seemingly effortless giving comes from a deep well of need. Here's how you can support them:

- **Initiate Intimacy:** Twos may struggle to express vulnerable needs – take the lead in creating spaces for emotional sharing.
- **Appreciate Effort, Not Just Results:** Focus on the intention behind their actions, not just the outcome.
- **Gently Challenge Avoidance:** Kindly point out when they are withdrawing or over-adapting, and encourage them to express themselves authentically.
- **Reassurance Goes a Long Way:** Tell them, and often, that you love them for who they are, not just what they do for you.

Finding True Connection

When a Type Two feels truly seen, known, and loved for exactly who they are, something magical happens – they relax. Their giving becomes less compulsive and flows from a genuine desire to share their warmth, not from a place of insecurity. And healthy intimacy offers the ultimate gift to a Helper – the profound realization that they didn't need to earn love after all; they were worthy all along.

THE GIFT OF EMPATHY: HOW TWOS CONNECT AND BUILD BRIDGES

If there's a superpower within the Enneagram, Type Twos wield the power of empathy. Their ability to tune into the emotions of others and intuitively understand their needs is nothing short of extraordinary. Yet, like any superpower, empathy, for a Helper, can sometimes be a double-edged sword.

Understanding Two-ish Empathy

The empathy of a Type Two is rooted in their Heart Center intelligence. It's a raw, visceral empathy – they don't just understand what someone is feeling, they feel it along with them. This deep connection allows them to offer comfort, support, and a sense of being truly understood.

Beyond mere understanding, Two-ish empathy carries a strong action-oriented component. It's as if there's a magnetic pull for them to ease another's pain. This manifests in actions big and small, from words of encouragement to taking on someone else's burdens in an effort to relieve their suffering.

The Joys of Empathy

A Helper's capacity for empathy enriches both their own lives and the lives of those around them. Benefits include:

- **Deep Connection:** Their ability to empathize is the bedrock of meaningful relationships, creating a sense of intimacy and fostering strong bonds.
- **Fulfilling Their Core Need:** Helping others in response to their empathy fulfills the Helper's desire to feel needed, loved, and appreciated.

- **Making a Difference:** Their ability to understand and ease the pain of others creates a sense of purpose and positive impact on the world.
- **Personal Growth:** Every empathic interaction is an opportunity to gain greater insight into human nature, expanding their own emotional intelligence.

The Challenges of Empathy

While the Two's empathy is a profound gift, it also carries unique challenges. These can include:

- **Emotional Burnout:** Absorbing the pain and struggles of others can lead to emotional exhaustion, compassion fatigue, and vicarious trauma.
- **Lost Boundaries:** Empathy makes it difficult to establish and maintain boundaries; Twos can become enmeshed with others' problems, neglecting their own needs.
- **Unrealistic Expectations:** A strong desire to fix and save can lead to frustration and a sense of helplessness when their efforts aren't met with the expected outcome.
- **Manipulative Tendencies:** Unhealthy Twos can use their empathy to manipulate situations or people, subtly positioning themselves as indispensable.

The Path to Balanced Empathy

The key for Twos lies in cultivating a healthy relationship with their empathy, using it as a guiding star without being consumed by it. Here's how:

- **Self-Awareness:** Recognizing when their empathy is becoming overwhelming and when they need to step back and recharge.
- **Stronger Boundaries:** Learning to set limits on how much emotional responsibility they take for others, practicing saying "no" with kindness.
- **Self-Care as Necessity:** Prioritizing their own emotional well-being, ensuring they have outlets to process their

feelings and refill their own cup of compassion.

- **Acceptance of Limitations:** Recognizing that they can't fix everyone or solve every problem, letting go of unrealistic expectations for themselves.

Empathy as a Bridge

A Two's empathy extends beyond one-on-one relationships. Skilled at reading the emotional tone of groups, they often excel at mediating conflict, finding common ground, and bringing people together. Their hearts are natural bridges, fostering understanding and cooperation.

The Fully Realized Helper

A Helper at their best recognizes that empathy is most powerful when balanced with self-preservation. They become beacons of compassion, offering support and understanding while maintaining their own emotional well-being. It's then that they can use their extraordinary gift of empathy to make the world a more connected, loving, and understanding place.

THE SHADOW OF PEOPLE-PLEASING: WHEN HELPING BECOMES UNHEALTHY

There's a dark underbelly to the Helper's natural generosity – a place where helpfulness transforms into harmful people-pleasing. When Twos operate from this shadow, their focus shifts away from genuine connection and towards gaining a fleeting sense of validation and approval.

Understanding People-Pleasing

People-pleasing is a way of manipulating situations and others to avoid potential rejection, conflict, or negative emotions. At its core lies the Two's fear of being unlovable or unwanted. Common people-pleasing behaviors include:

- **Saying "Yes" When You Mean "No":** Agreeing to requests or favors against their will to avoid disappointing others or appearing disagreeable.
- **Fawning:** Excessive praise, compliments, and flattery designed to win someone's affection or keep them happy.
- **Agreeing for the Sake of Harmony:** Passively going along with the group or opinions of others, silencing their true thoughts and feelings to avoid conflict.
- **Minimizing Own Needs:** Downplaying their desires, pretending not to be bothered by things, or focusing excessively on others' needs while neglecting their own.

Ironically, people-pleasing rarely results in the genuine connection a Helper craves.

The Vicious Cycle

The more Twos resort to people-pleasing, the deeper they cement a belief that their true self is not enough to earn love. Here's how the cycle unfolds:

1. **Fear of Rejection:** The underlying fear of not being good enough fuels the urge to perform in order to be liked and accepted.
2. **People-Pleasing Behavior:** This manifests in various ways, all designed to get external validation and avoid negative emotions.
3. **Temporary Relief:** A fleeting sense of being needed and liked arises, offering a false sense of security.
4. **Resentment Builds:** Underneath the surface, bitterness grows as they sacrifice their authenticity and needs for others.
5. **Self-Worth Declines:** Their own desires unmet, a sense of emptiness and a need for greater approval arises, further fueling the cycle.

Recognizing the Shadow of People-Pleasing

For Twos, it's important to distinguish healthy helping from its shadow form:

- **Healthy Helping:** Driven by genuine care and a desire to contribute; comes from a place of inner fullness and choice.
- **People-Pleasing:** Driven by fear and the need for external approval; leaves them feeling depleted and resentful.

The Path to Breaking Free

Escaping the people-pleasing trap is deeply intertwined with a Helper's journey to self-worth. Practices to consider:

- **Identifying Triggers:** What situations make you prone to putting others' needs above your own? Understanding the triggers brings awareness.
- **"No" as Self-Care:** Practice saying "no" in small ways. Remember, it's okay to disappoint others sometimes in order to honor yourself.

- **Tune Into Your Body:** When you feel the urge to people-please, notice your body. Is your stomach clenched? Are your shoulders tense? Your body provides clues to your true feelings.
- **Challenge Your Inner Critic:** Identify the negative self-talk that reinforces the belief that you must be agreeable to be lovable. Replace it with compassionate self-affirmations.
- **Seek Support:** Talking to a therapist or trusted friend can help you identify patterns, heal underlying wounds, and develop healthier coping mechanisms.

The Freedom of Authenticity

Breaking free from people-pleasing leads to a powerful realization: that genuine love and connection can only be built on authenticity. When a Two learns to honor their own needs, set boundaries, and express their truth, they paradoxically become more attractive to the right people.

While the shadow of people-pleasing can feel all-consuming, the Helper spirit is resilient. With self-awareness, practice, and immense compassion for themselves, Type Twos can shed the weight of trying to please everyone and discover the liberating joy of being their true, worthy selves.

LOVE AND OWNERSHIP: REDEFINING LOVE FOR THE HEALTHY TWO

Like a thirsty traveler in the desert, the Type Two Helper searches for the oasis of love. But what does real, nourishing love look like for someone whose identity is so closely intertwined with caring for others? Sadly, many Twos unconsciously perpetuate a belief that love must be earned, sacrificing their needs under the guise of generosity. Yet, there's another way, a path leading to the type of love that feeds the soul rather than depletes it.

Let's dissect the unhealthy Two's perception of love. They may confuse it with need – believing that the more intensely they need another person, the deeper their love. They may chase after constant affirmation, mistaking validation for genuine affection. Their love may become entangled with ownership – subtly seeking control within relationships as a way to guard against the gut-wrenching fear of abandonment.

This type of love can feel exhilarating at first, a whirlwind of intense emotions that fill their internal void. Yet, like a mirage, it proves unstable and ultimately unsatisfying. Why? Because this type of love depends on external forces, leaving the Helper vulnerable to fluctuations in another person's mood, attention, or approval. And, in focusing on what they can receive, they neglect the most important source of love of all – themselves.

The path to healthy love for a Two lies in a radical concept: they are inherently worthy. It's a challenging shift in perspective, one that requires confronting the deep-seated belief that who they are isn't enough. It's a process of unraveling a lifetime of confusing their value with their actions.

To begin this journey, a Two must first learn to recognize and care for themselves as they would care for another. Self-love isn't a selfish act, it's the foundation for a healthier understanding of what they deserve in any relationship. This involves learning to ask, "What do I need in this moment?" and honoring the answer. It is setting boundaries, communicating honestly, and allowing themselves to experience and express the full range of their emotions, not just the ones deemed acceptable or helpful.

Learning to love themselves in this way leads to a beautiful paradox. When Twos stop chasing external validation and begin filling their own cup, they create an inner wellspring of love that radiates outwards. Their giving becomes less about self-sacrifice and more about sharing their abundance. They become more discerning, attracting healthier relationships with those who see and appreciate their true value.

This doesn't mean Twos become cold or uncaring. Their genuine generosity and warmth simply flow from a different source. They discover that the capacity to love others deeply grows as their capacity to love themselves expands. They begin to recognize that love is a choice, not something earned in a constant exchange of favors. And with that knowledge comes true emotional freedom.

The healthy Two understands that reciprocal love exists, a flow of care and affection that doesn't keep score. They learn that healthy love allows space for both individuality and connection. Most importantly, they realize that to be fully loved by another, they must first fully love and accept all that they are, flaws included. And that's when the miracle happens: a love that doesn't own or control, but appreciates, supports, and cherishes the beautiful essence of a Helper's heart.

THE POWER OF BOUNDARIES: PROTECTING YOURSELF WHILE STILL HELPING OTHERS

The very idea of "boundaries" can feel foreign, even a little selfish, to the heart of a Helper. While their capacity for compassion is boundless, Type Twos often struggle to identify where they end and another person begins. This lack of clear boundaries can lead to emotional enmeshment, burnout, and the erosion of their own well-being. Yet, the truth is, setting boundaries is the ultimate act of kindness – one that both honors their own limitations and creates the space for healthier, more sustainable relationships.

First, it's important to understand why Twos often avoid boundaries. Deep down, they may fear that saying "no" or expressing their needs will lead to rejection or prove that they aren't truly lovable. They may subconsciously believe that their value lies in their willingness to set aside their own wants and desires completely. The reality is, healthy relationships thrive on balance. It is in the space between two individuals that genuine connection, freedom, and mutual respect can grow.

So, how does a Two learn to hold their ground while remaining true to their giving nature? It starts with a simple recognition: having needs is human, and your needs are important. It's giving yourself permission to pause, check in with yourself, and ask "Does this feel right for me?" before automatically agreeing to something. It's realizing that you can be caring and kind while still saying "no" to requests of your time, energy, and resources.

Learning to set boundaries is a practice, one that likely involves initial discomfort. You may feel a pang of guilt, a worry that someone will be disappointed. But it's through facing this discomfort that you build the vital muscle of self-advocacy. Start with small, less intimidating boundaries. Instead of accepting every last-minute favor, gently say, "I really wish I could, but I'm overcommitted right now." Instead of endlessly listening to a friend vent without offering a solution, redirect, "I so want to support you, and I'm also feeling overwhelmed. Can we check in again tomorrow?"

As you gain confidence, you'll discover that setting boundaries doesn't make you a bad Helper, it makes you a better one. The people who truly value you will respect your limits and support your need to care for yourself. Furthermore, having the space to recharge allows you to show up more fully and generously for others. It prevents the all-too-common slide from selfless to resentful.

There's also a profound shift in perspective that can aid Twos in embracing boundaries. Instead of interpreting another person's disappointment as a sign of your unworthiness, reframe it as giving them an opportunity to learn self-reliance. When you're always there to offer help, you may be unintentionally depriving others of the chance to discover their own strength and resilience.

Remember, it's not just about boundaries with others, but also boundaries with yourself. This includes respecting your physical limits, getting enough sleep, scheduling time for things you enjoy, and asking for help when you've reached your emotional capacity.

The journey with boundaries involves embracing imperfection. There may be times you slip back into old patterns, feel overwhelmed by guilt, or simply aren't sure how to proceed. It's okay. Be patient with yourself. The simple fact of becoming aware of your patterns is a significant step forward. Boundaries aren't walls that isolate you. They are protective structures that allow your heart to give from a place of authenticity and sustainable generosity.

THE HEAD IN THE CLOUDS:
WHEN THE FEELING
CENTER TAKES OVER

Type Twos wear their hearts on their sleeves. Their emotions are a compass, guiding their actions and defining their interactions with the world. But, as with all strengths, this deeply empathic nature also contains the seeds of vulnerabilities. When the Heart Center becomes all-encompassing, practical thinking, objectivity, and self-preservation can be swept aside.

Let's imagine the Enneagram centers of intelligence (Head, Heart, and Body) as characters vying for attention with the heart often taking the lead role. The Head – associated with logic, critical thinking, and detachment – can feel stifled by the Helper's insistent emotional focus. In times of stress particularly, Twos may find it near impossible to silence their emotional inner soundtrack, resulting in overthinking, impulsive decisions, and potential disregard for the sensible advice they'd readily offer a friend.

This tendency leaves them vulnerable to several unique challenges. First, they can become easily overwhelmed or blinded by their own emotions. Imagine a parent whose fear of their child failing obscures recognition of their child's resilience. Or, a Two so devastated by hurt feelings after a conflict that they overlook the bigger picture of a supportive friendship.

Secondly, strong emotions can warp the Two's perception of reality. An underlying fear of being unloved can make even neutral interactions feel like a dismissal. This tendency to personalize events makes it difficult to step back and gain an objective perspective, often fueling unnecessary worry and spiraling negative thought patterns.

Third, an over-reliance on their Heart Center can hinder a Two's ability to set healthy boundaries. Their focus on fulfilling the needs of others may override a rational recognition of their own limits. This is where the line between empathy and manipulation, while often subconscious, can become blurred. Their innate understanding of emotions can be used, sometimes even unintentionally, to gain a desired outcome in a situation.

So, how can a Two create a more harmonious symphony between their Head and their Heart? Integration with the types of the Head Center (Five, Six, and Seven) is key. This doesn't mean suppressing their emotions, but rather cultivating a healthy relationship with them. Practices that can help include:

- Mindfulness: Observing thoughts and emotions without judgment creates a spaciousness that lessens their immediate grip.
- Journaling: Writing out strong feelings puts them on "paper", allowing for more objective examination at a later time.
- Seeking Outside Perspective: Trusted friends or a therapist can act as a sounding board, offering a less emotionally-charged view of a situation.
- Stepping Away: Especially when big emotions arise, physically removing themselves gives Twos time for their emotional waves to subside, enabling clearer thinking.
- Balancing the Heart and the Body: Grounding practices like exercise, time in nature, or deep breathing can shift focus from the tumultuous mind-space into the steadiness of the body.

When a Two is able to tap into the wisdom of their Head, they move towards a healthier balance. They'll still be the warm, empathetic people they are, but with a dash of rational discernment that safeguards them from making decisions based solely on fear, neediness, or overwhelming emotion.

The ultimate gift of Head Center integration for a Two is the ability to hold their deep compassion alongside a clear understanding of reality. It's the shift from "I feel like they don't care", to "I feel hurt, and I also remember the many ways they've shown care in the past". The ability to navigate the world with both their warm heart and their grounded head leads to greater resilience, clarity in relationships, and the empowering realization that they don't need to be controlled by their feelings.

FROM CODEPENDENCY TO INTERDEPENDENCY: BUILDING HEALTHY SUPPORT SYSTEMS

"I need you." For Type Twos, this phrase is both a cry for connection and a potential trapdoor into codependency. Codependent relationships are often characterized by a focus on fixing, rescuing, or enabling another person, losing a healthy sense of self within that dynamic. It's a slippery slope for Helpers, whose deep-seated desire to be loved and needed can create a perfect storm for enmeshment.

Let's dissect why codependency is often the Two's shadow side. Their focus on the well-being of others can blur the lines between caring and controlling. They may derive a sense of purpose and validation from feeling indispensable, even if it means sacrificing their own well-being and delaying attention to their own unmet needs. Codependent relationships are fertile breeding grounds for people-pleasing, the suppression of negative emotions, and a gradual, but detrimental, erosion of boundaries.

Unhealthy support systems have cascading effects. When perpetually focused on others, Twos neglect their own internal world. It's a path that leads to resentment, emotional exhaustion, and an undernourished sense of self. They may develop an unhealthy reliance on another person as the primary source of their emotional validation. And worst of all, codependency rarely produces positive change as it removes personal accountability from the equation.

It's important to emphasize: the desire to help is not the problem, it's the way in which it sometimes manifests. The good news is, Twos can build healthy, supportive relationships without sacrificing themselves in the process. This journey begins with a simple yet profound shift: towards interdependency.

Interdependency values connection while preserving individuality. It's a balance of give and take, a sense of being there for each other that doesn't suffocate either person. Interdependent relationships are built on honest communication, healthy boundaries, and a celebration of growth, both as individuals and within the dynamic itself.

So, how does a Two cultivate more interdependent relationships? It involves several shifts in perspective and behaviors:

- Recognizing Codependent Tendencies: Identifying patterns of over-functioning, needing to be needed, and difficulty expressing negative emotions are the first steps towards change.
- Embracing Mutual Support: Healthy relationships offer care in both directions. Allow yourself to receive support, even in small ways, to reinforce that you are just as worthy of being cared for as others.
- Focus on Your Own Growth: Instead of pouring all your energy into "fixing" someone else, invest in your personal development. This strengthens your sense of self and makes you a healthier partner, friend, or family member.
- Open Communication: Practice talking openly about your own needs and desires. This includes the ability to set loving boundaries and express difficult emotions without fear.
- Letting Go of the Outcome: Recognize that you can support someone without controlling the result. True change comes from within, not from your external efforts.

Building interdependent relationships can feel vulnerable, a rewiring of old patterns. Be patient with yourself, and be selective when choosing those you let closest. Seek out those who appreciate your warmth but don't exploit it. Find people who support your growth journey, who challenge you to embrace your full self, and who demonstrate what a true, balanced connection looks like.

The path of a Two often involves untangling the concept of love from being needed. True love is a celebration of who you are, not dependency on who you can become for another person. As your understanding of support, connection, and healthy relationships expands, so will your inner sense of security. You'll discover the liberating freedom of caring from a full heart, one with a firm foundation within yourself.

THE INNER CRITIC'S VOICE: ADDRESSING SELF-DOUBT IN TYPE TWOS

Amidst the outpouring of love and support characteristic of Type Twos, there often hides a relentless inner critic. It's a voice fueled by the Two's core fear of being unlovable, a voice that whispers doubts, questions their worth, and magnifies any perceived failure in their quest to be helpful and caring. The constant striving to live up to their own impossibly high standards can lead to profound self-doubt and even a subtle feeling of inner shame.

This inner critic isn't always loud or overt. It can be a persistent undercurrent of thoughts like: "They don't really appreciate what I did," "I'm not good enough," or "I'm failing everyone". It's the voice that, after a warm interaction, finds a single negative comment to dissect and obsess over. It's the voice that magnifies mistakes within acts of kindness, distorting them into evidence of fundamental unworthiness.

Understanding the inner critic is crucial for a Two's growth. This critical voice has roots in their early experiences, where they may have internalized the message that love was conditional, that they had to earn affection by anticipating and exceeding the needs of others. This unconscious belief creates a fertile ground for self-doubt to thrive, a never-quite-good-enough feeling that propels their ceaseless effort to win the unwinnable battle for enduring validation.

Left unchecked, the inner critic becomes a tyrannical ruler, leading to several unhealthy consequences. First, relentless self-criticism erodes self-esteem. Even when others offer genuine praise, Twos struggle to internalize it, their inner critic always there to twist it into further "proof" that they're secretly an imposter. Second, it fuels people-pleasing and an unhealthy drive for perfectionism. Instead of acting from a place of genuine desire, their actions can become motivated by a fear of not being good enough and a constant need to silence the critic's voice.

The path towards liberation from the inner critic involves compassion, awareness, and a reframing of their deepest beliefs. Here are some strategies Twos can utilize:

- Identify Your Critic: Give your inner critic a name or persona. Separating it from your true self creates distance for observation. Notice its patterns, favorite phrases, and the situations that trigger it most.
- Challenge Your Critic: Question the truth of the critic's claims. Would you say those things to a friend? Search for evidence that counters the negative self-talk.
- Practice Self-Compassion: Talk to yourself with the same kindness you readily offer others. Replace the critic's harsh words with understanding and affirmations.
- Focus on the Intention: Remind yourself of the positive intentions behind your actions, even if the outcome wasn't perfect. Mistakes don't define your worth.
- Seek Support: Talking to a therapist or trusted friend can help you unravel the origins of your inner critic and develop a healthier inner dialogue.

Silencing the inner critic entirely is neither realistic nor desirable. It holds clues to a Two's deepest insecurities. Yet, Twos can learn to relate to this voice without being consumed by it. They can begin to view their inner world through the lens of compassion and understanding, recognizing that their inherent worth has never been dependent on perfection.

Taming their inner critic is essential for a Two's overall well-being. As their self-talk shifts from judgment to kindness, they develop a more solid inner foundation from which their generosity can sustainably flow. And, in those quieter moments, they might finally hear a different voice, one that whispers a truth they've carried deep within all along: "You are loved, simply for being you."

FROM SELFLESS TO SELF-AWARE: CULTIVATING SELF-CARE FOR THE HELPER

The idea of self-care can feel almost at odds with the Helper's identity. Prioritizing themselves may stir a pang of guilt, a worry that they're being selfish. Yet, paradoxically, the act of self-care is the key to a Helper becoming their most giving, impactful, and fulfilled self. It's the antidote to the potential pitfalls of emotional burnout, resentment, and an ever-shrinking sense of self.

Why do Twos often struggle with self-care? For starters, their deeply ingrained focus on others can create a blind spot when it comes to their own needs. They may also hold an unconscious belief that taking care of themselves first somehow diminishes their ability to care for others. Add in the inner critic, whispering that their wants are less essential than those around them, and you have a recipe for self-neglect. This leads to a slow erosion of their energy, enthusiasm, and that bright spark that makes them a Two.

Let's dissect the subtle shift from "selfless" to "self-aware". True selflessness isn't about ignoring yourself completely. It's recognizing that you can't pour from an empty cup. When Twos learn to replenish themselves, the quality of their giving transforms. It becomes sustainable, joyful, and devoid of the undercurrent of resentment that accompanies martyrdom.

So, how does a Helper integrate essential self-care? It starts with a simple recognition: your needs matter. This includes physical, emotional, and mental needs. And just as you wouldn't dream of depriving a child of food or sleep, you must grant yourself the same basic care.

Practical self-care might involve ensuring they get enough sleep, eat nourishing foods, and have some time for activities they enjoy. Emotional self-care includes practices like journaling, therapy, or carving out time to simply process difficult feelings, both their own and those they absorb from others. Mental self-care might look like setting aside "worry time" to combat overthinking, engaging in relaxation techniques, or allowing space for unstructured time to let their minds wander freely.

It's crucial for a Two to be honest with themselves about the kinds of self-care that truly nourish them. There's no point in forcing self-care activities that leave them feeling depleted or guilty (looking at you, obligatory bubble baths!). Pay attention to what actually fills your cup, even if it seems unconventional.

One of the greatest challenges is overcoming the feeling that self-care is an indulgence. Reframe it as an investment in your most valuable asset: the boundless generosity you offer the world. Remember, caring for yourself allows you to step away from the daily grind and reconnect with your inner essence, a reminder of why helping others brings so much joy in the first place.

For Twos who've dedicated so much to others, integrating self-care is a practice that takes time and compassion. Start small. If the idea of scheduling a whole day for yourself feels overwhelming, begin with 15 minutes of reading an enjoyable book. If carving out time feels impossible, pay attention to small ways to add moments of nourishment to your day – a soothing cup of tea, a mindful walk around the block, or a few minutes of undisturbed deep breathing.

As Twos embrace self-care, they discover that they're not only surviving but also thriving. They show up for others with more energy, greater patience, and a renewed sense of purpose. Ultimately, they realize that caring for themselves is not a selfish act, but the ultimate form of selflessness - the gift of giving their best, most vibrant self to those in the world.

THE GROWTH PATH: MOVING TOWARDS THE HEALTHY FOUR

The Enneagram is far more than just a personality categorization tool - it's a map for growth. For Type Twos, the path towards greater balance and integration lies in understanding their movement towards Type Four (The Individualist) in times of emotional security. Twos and Fours share a similar core focus on the inner emotional landscape, yet manifest this focus in unique ways.

Twos are drawn outward, projecting warmth and seeking validation in the external world. Fours turn inward, seeking a deep understanding of their own identity and a unique mode of self-expression. Yet, hidden within the warm, giving Helper is a yearning for the Four's authenticity and introspection.

Healthy Twos, in periods of security and well-being, naturally begin to tap into some of the positive characteristics of the Four, such as:

- Deeper Self-Awareness: They develop a richer understanding of their own emotional landscape, recognizing subtle nuances in their feelings and the underlying motivations behind their actions.
- Embracing Creativity: Twos may find themselves drawn to creative outlets, whether through artistic expression, journaling, or simply finding unique ways to add their personal touch to their daily lives.
- Acceptance of Negative Emotions: They move towards a healthier relationship with uncomfortable emotions like sadness, anger, and disappointment, allowing themselves to feel those fully without suppressing them or seeking immediate resolution.

- Focus on Identity: A curiosity about who they are beyond their role as Helper develops. They may start to explore their own unique interests, values, and preferences separate from those of the people they care for.

This integration is a beautiful thing for a Two. It allows them to honor the depths of their own individuality while maintaining their warmth and connection to the world. The Four's influence provides a counterbalance to the Two's tendency to lose themselves in the needs of others.

But this integration isn't always consistent. Stress can push Twos in the opposite direction, towards the less healthy qualities of Type Eight (The Challenger). In this movement, Twos may become more assertive, even confrontational, and may lose touch with their softer, more vulnerable side. Recognizing this pattern helps Twos become more mindful and choose a conscious path towards their integration point.

So, how can Twos actively nurture their Fourish qualities? Here are some practices to consider:

- Introspection: Make time for quiet reflection, journaling about emotions, and asking inward-focused questions like "What truly brings me joy?"
- Alone Time: Create non-negotiable periods of solitude for recharging. This allows space away from the external pull the Two knows so well.
- Expressing the Unsaid: Practice vocalizing the full spectrum of emotions, even when it feels uncomfortable, moving away from the Two's habit of putting a positive spin on everything.
- Celebrating Uniqueness: Embrace preferences that diverge from others. Choose the restaurant YOU enjoy, wear the outfit that sparks YOUR interest, express an opinion that might differ.

Remember, growth for a Two is not about becoming less giving or caring. It's about honoring the rich complexity within themselves. The integration of Four qualities fosters a deeper sense of authenticity, creativity, and the freedom to show up as their true, multifaceted selves. They discover that connecting with their own unique individuality enhances, rather than diminishes, their ability to connect with and support others. And who knows, in the process, they might even stumble upon a few hidden talents!

THE EMPOWERED HELPER:
LIVING A LIFE OF SERVICE
AND FULFILLMENT

As a Type Two progresses on their journey of growth, they move toward an empowered and fulfilling version of themselves. It's a transformation where their desire to help doesn't exhaust or diminish them, but instead fuels them. They maintain their warmth and generosity, but from a place of inner strength, healthy boundaries, and a well-developed sense of self. They begin to live the fullest expression of their Helper archetype.

So, what does an empowered Helper look like? They embody several key shifts in both their internal and external worlds:

- Healthy Love: They understand the difference between giving from a place of fear and giving from a full heart. They recognize that love doesn't need to be earned, embracing their inherent worthiness of care and connection.
- Balanced Boundaries: They become skilled at saying "no" with kindness and maintaining the limits they need for their own well-being. They create space to recharge and replenish, recognizing this is what allows them to be their most giving selves.
- Authentic Connection: They form healthy relationships based on reciprocity, honesty, and respect. They no longer feel compelled to morph themselves into what they think others need, but can be their full, genuine selves within relationships.
- Integration of the Head: Their decisions are grounded in a balance of heart and logic. They can step back from overwhelming emotions and access the objectivity needed for clear decision-making.

- Self-Compassion: Their inner critic softens, replaced by a voice of understanding. They recognize their flaws as human and extend to themselves the same kindness they freely give to others.
- Discerning Helpfulness: They learn the difference between helping and enabling. They continue to offer support, but recognize the importance of allowing others to find their own strength.
- Embracing Joy: It's not just about fulfilling needs, but finding joy in the simple moments of connection, creativity, and self-expression. They give themselves permission to receive pleasure as readily as they provide it for others.

The path of growth is ever-unfolding for a Two. There will be times when they revert to old patterns, feel consumed by their emotions, or struggle to set boundaries. That's okay. The commitment to personal development, fueled by self-compassion, is what separates a stagnant Two from an empowered one.

As they embrace this path, they discover a beautiful truth: their growth benefits not only themselves but everyone they touch. Their healthier presence naturally uplifts others, modeling authenticity and self-respect. Their ability to hold space, listen deeply, and empower rather than fix transforms their relationships and their way of moving through the world.

The empowered Helper is no longer driven solely by deep needs, although their empathy remains a powerful force. Their giving comes from a place of joy and overflow. They've discovered the secret: that in caring well for yourself, you create the capacity to care for others with even greater abundance.

Most importantly, this journey leads to an inner peace that no amount of external validation can match. They recognize that their worth doesn't hinge on any person or action, but rests solidly within the gentle and unwavering heart of who they are. It is from this solid foundation that their gift of empathy, combined with self-awareness, empowers them to move through the world with grace, making a positive impact that echoes long after their actions. The empowered Two is a beacon of light, reminding us all of the profound strength found within a truly generous heart.

www.ingramcontent.com/pod-product-compliance
Lightning Source LLC
Chambersburg PA
CBHW051714250726
48653CB00007B/3023